A Fine-Tuned Heart

A Fine-Tuned Heart

New Poems by Don Gutteridge

2022

First Edition

Wet Ink Books
www.WetInkBooks.com
WetInkBooks@gmail.com

A Fine-Tuned Heart
New Poems by Don Gutteridge

Cover Design – Richard M. Grove
Layout and Design – Richard M. Grove

Typeset in Garamond
Printed and bound in Canada
Distributed in USA by Ingram,
    – *to set up an account* – *1-800-937-0152*

Library and Archives Canada Cataloguing in Publication

Title: A fine-tuned heart / new poems by Don Gutteridge.
Names: Gutteridge, Don, 1937- author.
Identifiers: Canadiana 20230168086 | ISBN 9781989786802 (softcover)
Classification: LCC PS8513.U85 F46 2023 | DDC C811/.54—dc23

Contents

Symphonic

I sit at ease in my rocker,
84 years young, SYM
still able to breathe
in my old bones, listening
to Peter, Paul and Mary
sing the songs of the long-
ago Sixties, that brought
the blood up and wakened us
to the world, or stung our cherub-
cheeks with tears that such
glorious chording, such
disarming harmonies,
such melodious musing
should be un-lunged
and bloom anew in our ears
like a seven-sea-ed symphony,
letting us know we are human
after all, and Heaven is nothing
but a fine-tuned heart.

The Ogle of My Eye

For Grace Leckie

Grace Leckie, the ogle
of my eye, spotting an auto
whizzing past the school,
would shout, "He's goin' to beat
sixty," and then mention
yet again that her brother,
old enough to drive
the family bus, could better
that by five and leave
the doubters in the dust – and I thought
of my Dad in our ancient 'Olds,
that baulked at forty and coughed
to a stop, like a ruptured rhino,
but Grace had freckles that left me
wheezing at the knees, and I
could have listened all day
just to hear her spout,
with two licks of her luscious
lip, "He's goin' to beat sixty."

O Tom!

For Tom in loving memory

O Tom! Please know
that I have done with weeping,
I wept till my bones bled
and then wept again,
but the pain pulsed anew,
unappeased, but now
I am at ease with God's
guile and the grief of your going,
for I have let you settle
in the consoling abode of my heart,
where your soul sings me to sleep,
brings some solace on,
and bids me believe you haven't
gone.

Chalk and Cheese

Tommy and Glen Fahselt
were chalk and cheese, the former
my blue-eyed, freckled
friend, the latter a genial
bully, and O how I envied them
their brand-new, British
built three-speeds
with handle-bar brakes
(which would have to do them
till their Dad remembered
who they were), and Glen
eased the rage that seethed
inside, orphaned and unappeased,
by throwing me facedown,
straddling my back, and slowly
squeezing the breath from my body,
and when he rolled away,
and my death was postponed,
he was laughing, unbothered
by the twinge of my tears,
and my thought was: at least
I've got a father.

Max's Taxi

Sarnia Township: 1947-1949
For Max Laur: In Memoriam

When the winter chill dipped
below the 'old' zero
and school was still a gelid
mile away, we made straight
for the sisters Laur and Max's
taxi: half-a-ton
or so of shivering tin
that had to be cranked into
balky submission, and while
Bob sat smugly in back
between the girls and their giggles,
I rode shotgun, hunched
in the meagre heat of the engine's
judder, and waiting for the cold
crunch of gears and the first
grumpy chug of motorized
motion – and Max's triumphal
laugh that made it all worthwhile.

Peony

Chatham, Ontario: June, 1954

Our barren backyard,
where the grass grew in grudging
clumps, was garnished by a single,
solitary bush, teeming
with peonies in the salubrious
ooze of a June afternoon,
whose petals were as purple
as the Pope's robes, where ants
as black as cracked walnuts
busied themselves with pollen
and procreation, and as I
trundled our second-hand
mower to and fro
like a muffled metronome
over the rumpus of our lawn
with one eye glued to the
frothed blossoms, I wondered
who had thought enough
of beauty to plant it here
for me to espy, and prompt
this poem.

The Tug of Touch

For Tom in loving memory

How many wintry evenings
when the dark was young enough,
did we play at "Lunker," the piscatory
game I invented just
for us – to reprise some
wonder of our summering days
on Cameron, where we angled for
rainbow or behemoth bass,
with a Daredevil's darting
or a Wobbler's* crippled ripple,
or happily settled for a
fistful of perch, and our love
grew without the luxury
of words or the tug of touch,
and the afternoons passed
as soothing as a loon, alight
on a lake, uncaring
that nothing, not even love,
lasts.

Daredevils and William's Wobblers:
fishing lures or plugs

Barely Five

For Tim

You were barely five,
your blue eyes lit with the
lustre of just being new
in the now, and we played in the
sand-box I built
for you in the shade of the old
garage, like a couple of bumptious
pups, and whenever I soaked
enough sand to make
a moated castle, you smacked it
flat with a golden grin
that has lasted more than
thirty years and kept
the kid alive inside
the man.

Fancy-Fed

Whenever I want my fancy
fed, I merely close
my eyes and dream of the day
when Coop, the gang and I
set out to find what lay
beyond the unmarred dark
of Bob Leckie's bush,
long forbidden terrain,
and I felt like LaSalle with his sights
on some Mississippi
in his mind, as we breeched the
tree-flumed gloom
and let its shadows shiver
the shade – and whistling a Natty
Bumppo tune, I led
my intrepid troops into the
sunshine on the other side,
rinsing a derelict windmill,
flapping its blades in the breeze,
and no-one among us
needed a map or illustrated
guide to tell us we'd found
ourselves a genuine buccaneer's
barque in full sail –
abloom in the boy-soil
of our mutual imagination.

Legendary

The legend of the Reverend Bell's
near eclipse with a lit
match and gas was licorice
to every lip in the village,
and the prurient soon made
a pilgrimage to appraise the hedge,
where the blast had parked the parson's
arse, and from which.

Dead-Man's-Float

Canatara: July 1947

At eleven, I was still a non-
swimmer, but had mastered
the dead-man's-float,
and that summer Sunday
when the morning was as warm as the
noontide high, I begged
Grandpa to take me to the beach
and the shimmering shallows beyond,
and we arrived in the wheezing
heat: me in my skin-thin
trunks and he in his second-
best suit and polished
oxfords, and while he watched
like a Coldstream Guard,
I let my body unbend
the chill, and cast an eye
upon a far sandbar
and the ten-foot deep
between us, and, face-first
and proudly prone, I scissor-
kicked till my toes bottomed
and my chin rose in triumphant
repose, but even at this remote,
I could see my Grandpa looking
grim, and remembered then:
he couldn't swim.

Ribald

For Bobby Cooper

Coop and I made it
a point of pride to ogle
every girl on Canatara,
and in particular those
in one-piece suits
that clung to their curves like silk
on a belly-dancer's hip –
whenever they emerged from the cold
blue element or when a
rogue wave soaked them
through and stiffened their nipples
enough to make us dream
of sidling up and giving
one of them a ribald
nibble.

Cosseted

Sarnia Township: 1949

The field behind our country
school was a lapsed pasture,
its sun-lashed grasses
corralled by a chicken-pen
fence, unbarbed and breeze
brushed, and we dallied there
in its ample ambit, as cosseted
as bunnies in their burrow, and O
how we sped when the wind
was a-lee, my rugby birthday
ball tossed from palm
to palm just to feel the ounce
in its bounce, and the girls galloping
with us, long-legged
in the flounce of their frocks – and there was
no-one to remind us that clocks
ticked and that our hickory-
docked world might come
undone.

Gerry

Chatham, Ontario: circa 1953

I often heard my father
disparage the Jews, even though
the only one he knew
was his tailor, Louis Berger,
who let him lay away
a ten-dollar suit
he wore at his wedding, and he averred
that they talked with their hands,
and hinted they were more clannish
than mannish, but when I finally
encountered an example, it was
Gerry Cohen, the class
cutup, whose outlandish antics
made us laugh a lot
and kept our teachers honest,
and often I was laughing so hard
I didn't have time to notice
whether his hands were moving
or not.

Broth without Bread

Mabel Foster wasn't old
and didn't live in a shoe,
but she had more children
than the storybook Mum
with much ado, and let them
litter our streets like flotsam
from her flesh, clad only
in their undies when the weather
weakened, and when it didn't,
wrapped in rags some
nosy neighbour had tossed,
and even then, I sensed
there was no happy ending,
that Jack would fall down
and Jill, unlaughing, after,
and all the king's horses
and his mighty men couldn't
put people together
again, and underfed kids
would have broth without bread.

Toggled

When ice cream was a nickel
a cone or a dime for double-
dipped, and arrived in three
dreamy colours, I thought
that "vanilla" was just a fancy
word for "white," and wondered
why "chocolate" and "strawberry"
didn't deserve the same
lofty treatment, referring
as they did to their humdrum
hues, but back then,
too young still
to tell "whether" from "why,"
the world came at us
piecemeal and agog,
leaving us to unpuzzle
its pied propensities
and toggled logic.

Machinery

We boys thought we knew
all about the push
and shove of love, and the
giddiness of the girlish id,
and had a rough idea
of the block and tackle required
to move the machinery,
but no notion of romance
with its coded tactics and niggling
niceties, or the joys of its slow
implode.

Left Hook

Point Edward: 1946

Still hoping, my Dad
buys me boxing gloves
for my birthday, and we shadow-
box for a while: him: bobbing
and weaving like Jersey Joe,
letting his chin jut
like a pugilist's prize I never
land a punch on, and so
we switch roles and my nose
becomes a butt for his rat-a-
tat jabs, and he pauses then
to show me how to keep
my guard up and be wary
of the low-blow or the mean
left hook, and I feel
good enough to try
my luck, fair means
or foul, in Bones Saunders'
jerry-rigged ring
against Oscar Crevier,
bigger than me and a tot
braver, and I am chagrined
when my chin chucks it in
and my second throws in the towel.

Kissing Cousins

Point Edward: 1945

Gerry's Dad came home
from the wars and the tail-gunning
of Huns with something
wounded and wary inside,
and tried to drink himself
into a more livable oblivion,
and before his heart gave up,
he sired a second son,
and, calling on Gerry
one day, I was surprised
to find his Mum's tummy
realigned, and my Gran
opined that he might've guzzled
enough booze to do
him in before kindling
fresh kin, and I wondered
even then, whether the
welter of war and its off-
kilter killing roused
in him the need to breed
and people the world
with kissing cousins.

Roguish

When Jo-Anne dropped her drawers
in the heathen heat of Hendries'
henhouse, all eyes
were ogled on the puckered pouch
that kept her thighs from colliding,
but when she suggested a roguish
reciprocity, we jostled
our jewels and debouched.

Rules

Point Edward: 1946

My friend Butch, had a theory
that the snakes he killed (because
they let their venom drool
on his shoes) came back to life
at midnight, including the one
twisting in the grass ahead
he'd clubbed to oblivion with his fake
shillelagh, and we watched its skin
quiver and start to stiffen
in the cooling breeze, and as
my horror began to show,
Butch averred, "No worries,
the night will tell," but when
we returned the very next day,
the creature lay where we left it,
un-venomed and very much dead,
and Butch said with an indifferent
shrug, "Some garters
don't know the rules."

Elixirs

For Anne in loving memory

O how we loved the songs
of the Sixties, when the world was new
and our love, young: tunes
like lissome-lunged Mary's
haunting hundred miles;
Dylan's troubadour buglings;
Paul's soaring solos
and Lennon's elliptica lines;
golden-voiced Gordon
in the early-morning rain,
Loretta's unforgettable
country gumption and sultry
serenades; Patsy going
crazy with the lyric tic;
The Rolling Stones gathering
no moss or satisfaction; -
and I listen one more time
to these reminiscing elixirs,
weep for what was and all
that's been lost, and husband
our love.

Bottled

For Tommy Fahselt: In Memoriam

Tommy leads me into the
little barn for the first
time, the morning chill
making balloons out of the
cows' breath, and the odour
of manure stings thru the straw
tossed on top, and gingerly
I take the proffered tines
and try my hand at mucking out
till my muscles buckle, and then
the main event begins:
as Tommy squats on a three-
legged stool beside
a tawny-mottled Guernsey

Beauty Bursts Us

We let our senses drown
in the sunlight that flares
in a flower or the dark that stuns
the stars awake, and we leave
our hearts open to the slow
imploding of an ode or the
Siren subtleties of song,
while the brushstrokes of a Van Gogh
or the marble musings of a
Michelangelo unsettle
our sight and skew the world
new, and Ludwig's Ninth
or Brahms' First, like endangering
angels, can stir in us
something too brittle
for the blood – nonetheless
we let it root and consume
because Beauty bursts us.

Hectic

I'd like to write a poem
that plumbed something too
hectic to be healed,
or perhaps an ode with Keatsean
teeth and iambic bones,
or a ballad that gallops with grit
in its rhymes to sing of daemon-
lovers undone by chance
or the world's wit, and knights-
at-arms, alone and loitering,
lily-browed, or pentameters
that dance aloud like the
Bard's, and bloom cathartic
in the heart, but whenever
I think of all the poems
inked upon the vellum
of the universe, I let my words
have their own say:
plumed and unbenumbed.

Wounds

Point Edward: 1945-48

A stone's throw from Grandfather's
house, I counted seven
alcoholics: *Charlie* next-door,
wounded by the War where it didn't
show till he'd downed a dozen
drafts; *Bob* over-the-road,
unhappy with his lot, staggered
home to beat his wife;
young *Murph*, who sired
more kids he didn't want
and welcomed beer's oblivion;
tail-gunner *Bill,* who drank
to drive the heebie-jeebies
from his dreams; *Easten,* who found
more solace in booze than his
doldrum days in the grocery;
Ross around-the-corner,
gutted by grief at the loss
of his toddler, sipped whiskey
till the pain drained; and *Harry,*
who still heard the big guns
above the Somme like an echo
only drink could deafen;
and how many more, unknown
to me, might there have been,
swigging alone in empty
rooms to find courage enough
to curse the God that made them.

Embraided

Chatham, Ontario: 1953
For my brother, Bob, in loving memory

A school-chum got
my brother and I and three
of his buddies hired on
hoeing beans in the slow
summer sun, and the big
bluff farmer in charge
handed us hoes and pointed
to the weed-seething rows
that needed our sweat and attention,
and when we'd chopped up
enough bull thistle
for him to spot the shirkers
and misfits, he settled his appraising
gaze on Bob's bright,
embroidered shirt, and snarled,
"Get your pay and go,"
and I should've taken Bob
in a brotherly embrace and stomped him
off the property without a
backward glance at that limp-
lidded, homophobic face –
but I didn't.

Tried and True

Miss Nelson did her best
to wean us away from saying
"Th' saft," when "this afternoon"
would nicely do, but our tongues,
though young, clung
to the tried and true, grafted
to the hackneyed past, eschewing
the new.

Blithe Spirit

Point Edward: 1946
For six-year-old Effie Free: In Memoriam

She was a blithe spirit,
her little body forever
in motion, as if her bones
needed to roam and her legs
move in lithe leaps,
and she was halfway between
her house and Hilliers soda
shop, when, musing more
about the lush gushing
of ice cream than where
she ought to be, she never
saw the car that struck her
down and left her lying
in the street like a dropped doll,
and did she, beyond the pain,
murmur, "Do I still get my treat?"

Enunciation

Point Edward: 1945

Long before I consented
to be born, Monk Street
was doubled in size to make
room for trolley-tracks
and a train-ride from village
to town, but because no auto
actually accosted the road,
it was decided to build a Victory
Garden between the boulevards,
and every morning en route
to school, I passed them by:
floral tributes to the lamented
dead, their remembering blooms
forever in season, but once
in a while, when Summer surprised
or the wind was right, I was sure
I could hear a trolley's trumpeting
enunciation

Bounce

Point Edward: Circa 1946

Many a Summer's day,
when the sun was as soft as new-
bee-ed honey, did Butch
and I, riding double
and flouting the Law, canvas
the road-side grasses
and wayside weeds for the
slightest sign of abandoned
bottles, tossed like flotsam
by careless imbibers, whose two-
penny empties would net us
a grab-bag: with four
blackballs, three
"I Love You" lozenges
and a pink thumb of bubble-
gum, and it was a red-
letter day when some
over-moneyed soul
jettisoned a five-cent
prize that paid for a
twelve-ounce Pepsi,
two straws and a bounce
in our step.

Rapture

My high-school teachers
were not passionate pedagogues,
but they passed muster with the likes
of us, unmarred by cognitive
thought or curiosity —
Miss Rowley, who could recite
Virgil as if it were the
local lingo, whose right
eye roved whenever
she scowled; Miss Carter,
a lump shy of retirement,
could be heard wheezing on the stairs
one wheedling step
at a time, blaspheming in flawless
French; Mr. Orr,
whose voice shook as he told us
the tale of a bookish bombardier,
coned above Cologne,
like a mesmerized moth;
Mr. Bond, whose big
voice boomed Geography
two rooms away;
Mr. Marcy, whose tutoring
technique was terror first,
learning later; Chester
Anderson, whose chemist's vestment
was Bunsen-burned and acid
spattered; and Miss Wilson,
who let me ransack her library
for Biggles' high-flying
sorties, that gave me
a lifelong itch for fiction
and the rapture of reading.

Why

Sarnia Township: 1951

My dog, Moochie,
was a water spaniel with webbed
paws that offered him
locomotion, should he ever
find himself up to his ears
in a lake, but anything that ebbed
and flowed gave him pause,
even the twitch-grassed
ditch that bordered his bailiwick,
but once on the road and pebbled
underfoot, he assailed every
upstart auto that passed
his way, like a rebel with a cause,
conniving to clamp his doggy
jaws on the offending wheel
and its impudent whirl or stun it
still with the baleful baying
of his bark, and O how I recall
the misted mornings when he trailed us
to school a mile away, like a hound
on a hare's drool, and settled
himself on the sun-warmed
porch till a pooch-loving
pupil tossed him a crust
or half-eaten apple,
and I remember, too, the day
distemper struck, and his puzzled,
pleading eyes, and the afternoon
my father dropped him off
on some empty acre
of the countryside – my wondering
where he was, and why.

Fuss

On Sunday summer evenings,
when the heat is heathen-deep,
the big front doors
of the Gospel Hall were flung
wide to let what little
breeze there was breathe
between the pews, and Gerry
and I, crouched beside
the stoop, listened in
to their Sabbath shenanigans,
hoping to hear them
talking-in-tongues some
biblical gibberish or Holy-
Roll up and down
the sanctified aisles –
just to please Jesus
or save their sinning souls,
but we wondered aloud if Heaven
itself was worth such a fuss.

Monkey's Uncle

When I was young enough
to believe that bards might be,
I tried to capture, in the
weave of words, some
thought that had never before
been thunk, but all that came out
of my minstrel's mouth was a clutter
of cliché and a chorus of
"I'll be a monkey's uncle."

Shine

For Sunday School, we had
to shine our shoes till the leather
lit, and we donned the duds
reserved for Sabbath shenanigans:
store-bought trousers
with a lean crease, a brand-
new shirt, its collar
stiffened by starch, a part
in our hair, pomaded and combed
till the roam surrendered,
and I wondered out loud
whether the Lord would slam
His Pearly Gates shut
on scuffed brogues or pleat-
depleted hopefuls too
hirsute to salute or stuffed
shirts unable to bend
their heads in penitent prayer –
but as soon as we opened our hearts
and sang "Jesus Loves Me,"
to the far coigns of the Choir,
we knew we would be loved,
rudely clothed, or nicely
nude.

Bounce

Point Edward: Circa 1946

Many a Summer's day,
when the sun was as soft as new-
bee-ed honey, did Butch
and I, riding double
and flouting the Law, canvas
the road-side grasses
and wayside weeds for the
slightest sign of abandoned
bottles, tossed like flotsam
by careless imbibers, whose two-
penny empties would net us
a grab-bag: with four
blackballs, three
"I Love You" lozenges
and a pink thumb of bubble-
gum, and it was a red-
letter day when some
over-moneyed soul
jettisoned a five-cent
prize that garnered us
a twelve-ounce Pepsi,
two straws and a bounce
in our step.

Ukelele

I never wanted to play
the ukulele like my Dad,
or sing like Bing, crooning
to the moon, or be as cocky
as the "Rocket" glowering down
a goalie, or impress a freckled
face, or run away from home
to a Barnum-and-Bailey gig,
or keep the Sabbath holy,
but O how I yearned
to find the Why in the words
that trammeled frantic inside
like a Dionysian dirge
I might, someday, assuage
on the white bit of the page.

Minuet

Home from school with a presumptive
cough, and slumped on Gran's
couch, I let the voices
from the dining-room radio
float and fathom: Helen
Trent's fraught romance,
Portia facing life alone,
the second Mrs. Burton
wishing she'd been the first,
Doctor Malone, too young
to be one, the hectic happenings
on Hilltop House, poor
plain Bill, that Dallas
gal, Stella, and her pal
Sunday, Pepper Young's
progeny, and the life and loves
of Lorenzo Jones with its swinging,
jigging intro – and I wondered,
between coughs, just
how many adults danced,
lovelorn, in fifteen-minute
minuets.

Riding Double

For Butch McCord: In Memoriam

My best friend, Butch,
rode a brand-new
C.C.M.
as sleek as a serpent's slither
and built for sprocketing speed,
and, riding double into the
belly of the breeze and thumbing
our noses at troublesome trees,
we prayed that Constable Peadon,
our resident bobby-in-blue,
would follow us wherever
we sped with his flat-footed,
slack-jawed trot,
and I didn't know what I enjoyed
the most: the bounce of my bottom
on the bike's scarlet bar,
or mocking the law.

Plimsoll

For Cap Harness: In Memoriam
Point Edward: 1945

Seven superannuated
"captains" roamed the Point,
and I knew them by the toppers
they sported as they ambled by
on their way to the morning post,
and I wondered how old Cap
Garvey, who nodded now
and then, had ever weathered
the Great Storm of ought-
thirteen, when waves on the
biggest lake hummocked
like mountains and the
Edmund Fitzgerald succumbed –
and when the winds had weakened
and the sun shone again,
the skipper's hair was withered
white, and then there was Cap
Beaten, down the street,
who'd harrumphed the *Hamonic*
away from the blazing pier,
ran it aground and watched it
burn to the plimsoll line,
and on any given day,
among the ghosts of souls
drowned in the Lake's wake,
sailors from a docked frigate
might be seen airing
their bell bottoms on the main
drag, and everyone I knew
called our breezy barber
"Cap," because, they said,
between snips he must've been
dreaming of blue-brimmed
horizons and sea-shouldering
ships.

Long After

Long after I am dead
and gone, the world will weary
on – with mini-wars
breaking blood here
and there or wherever there's
a where, or mammoth guns
need gamins to gut,
and tinpot potentates
with bigshot notions
connive, and Honest Abes
pledge to keep the Sabbath
holy, and sun-spun
days alleviate the rain,
and poems are penned to palpitate
on the page and bring their honey-
peace to bear, and love
will find an unsung niche
in which to thrive and plunder-
pluck despair.

Gilded

In the Point in those days,
there were, along Monk,
two Missus Shaws,
sisters who'd married brothers
when husband-material was un-
abundant, and love, in-lawed
or not, was where you found it,
and their modest cottages
faced one another across
the intervening street,
as if the nuptialled couples
needed to keep their cloisters
close, and though the Lord
did not bless them with children,
they never failed – sweeping
the summer's dust from their bordered
boulevard sand humming
all the while – to wave
as I passed them by,
and toss me a gilded smile.

Sting

Point Edward: 1946

Many an evening did we
watch in troubled awe
as the butcher's brother staggered
towards home, glassy-
eyed, from the Balmoral,
beverage room, where beer
was a nickel-a-pop, and the waiter
slinging it, did and often,
and, as always, Gran
and I on the front verandah
braced for the slap that shivered
windows and flinched a village,
delivered by a man unhappy
with God's allotment, and needing
some cheek meek enough
to take the sting out of it.

Detasseled

Chatham, Ontario: August 1952

It was August-hot, the sun
brooded above us, and the corn
grew in tall green
grooves, its tassels tossed
like golden gauze, and the big
beef-cheeked farmer
pointed to them, and said,
with a mischevious grin,
"Just think of 'em as your dink,
and pull," and off we sped
down the gendered rows,
gelding their pollen-rich
pizzles, and letting our sweat
gel in the heaving breeze,
happy to be here, flung
young, and unhasseled
by the tyrannies of Time or the flawed
optics of thought.

Thumbs

O to be that boy again!
to befuddle in puddles the rain
bequeaths and the sun shuns,
and feel their mud-luscious
shudder on our greedy, kneading
thumbs, and play away
the halcyon days at potsies
off-the-wall (cat's-eyes,
the prize) or jump-rope
till our pulses plump,
or bounce-a-ball to please
the girls and their awkward gawking,
or loping along in the wind's
ease, just to let
our feet find the secret
of their equilibrium and let
our breathing seethe inside
the stunned thunder of our lungs –
but – what once was
is always becoming, and joy,
however bright, is what's left
in the embers of our ripe
remembering.

Flouting

Grace was the girl two
rows over, with pigtails
that jiggled jaunty and buddings
that bevelled her blouse, who.
on sunny Saturdays, galloped
on by, aboard her chestnut
charger, thighs astride
and pummeled by the pommel,
(horse and rider in brute
embrace) – like Lady Godiva
flaunting her body.

Dance Fancy

Point Edward: 1946

In those days, people
couldn't afford fancy
artisans from the City to paper
over a bedroom wall
or two, but Missus-Shannon-
across-the-road would nicely
do, and besides, she'd let us
watch her smooth manoeuvres
and brush-touch, and I loved
the way she unspooled the roll
along the treselled table,
as slick as a toad's tongue
tasting a fly, or applied the paste
in sluiced swoops with a besom
big enough to paint
a brigantine's bottom, and when
she reached the ceiling, and had
to stand without a wiggle
or a wobble, her down-
side up and flying blind
to keep the blooms aligned,
I waited for the smile that seemed
to say, "I don't dance fancy,
but I get the job done."

Chrysalids

Sarnia Township: 1951

Coop preferred the tractor,
riding its troubled clutch
with a tiptoe touch, and guiding
the hiccoughing hulk and its racked
wagon between the stooked
sheaves of ripened wheat
like a sure-footed chauffeur,
while I was partial to the taut
tug of the reins in my farmhand's
grip, and the gentle jigging
of the matched Percherons, who needed
no nudging to thread their way
through the sweat-whetted men,
tossing their tined bundles
aboard – and while Coop motored
and I moseyed, we were spun
lovely in the summer-sun
like chrysalids cocooned, as if
we might be freed from the
soulless cycle of the seasons.

Low-Growing

For Bobby Cooper

That July when we packed up
our belongings and fled
to the far countryside
(where bees hummed a little
louder and birds brimmed
with a surfeit of summer song),
there were no school-
chums yet to befriend,
and kid-pickings were slim
(I counted but four abodes
within hailing distance
that might harbour one
or more lads like me:
still striving to shave
and hoping the girls wouldn't notice,
but did), and what relief,
when I'd come uncocooned
long enough to meet
the neighbour's boy and find
he didn't bite, and learned
that friendship, like love,
is a slow-growing delight.

Nosegay

The Widow Bray, to ease
her bereavement pain, fills
her garden with remembering blooms:
blood-bright tulips
to remind her of Spring's soothing
renewal and love's honeyed
beginning; day-lilies
to celebrate June and the burgeoning
of bees; glads and callas
to grace a husband's grave
when August draws the Summer
down; and button-roses
to see September out
and plant a nosegay on her grief.

Budding Stud

Sarnia Township: 1949

I follow Marilyn and the sisters
Laur into her stable
to watch the resident stallion
"cover" his first mare,
and we notice he's ready to roll:
his pincering instrument as red
as a ripened rose and bigger
than an embalmed salami, and while
the sisters titter and Marilyn
is merely amused, the budding
stud straddles his inamorata
like an underrehearsed acrobat
and buries his sizzling implement
in the mare's mallow with stiff-
legged thrusts that leave
the girls a-gasp at such a
lacerating passion, and me
to wonder aloud about the
limits of lust, and us.

Summer Saturday

Point Edward: 1948

It was a summer Saturday
when I teetered on the edge of
Mara's verandah and "called for"
Gerry, thinking betimes
of his sister: the dark halo
of her hair, eyes that leapt
lustrous from their lashes,
and a smile promising more,
"He's not home," came
a familiar voice from the outdoor
privy, its double-doors
shockingly open to expose
Nancy, squatted on the potty,
her undies slumped below,
and while I was looking for a place
to hide, the dance in romance
died.

The Day I Almost Drowned

Point Edward: July, 1947

Nancy and Gerry Mara
could swim like slim-finned
dolphins or sleek-thrashing
salmon, in the full-fathomed
Slip, where drowning was ever
imminent, or the underwater
dells of the Great Lake
(where they gave my dog-paddling
dithers a compassionate glance),
and I was tucked safely
ashore on the morning they dared
to circumnavigate the frothing
waters of our derelict pier,
whose jagged spiles bred
impromptu eddies or quick-
fisting whorls, and I watched them
with envious awe until they
rose from the foam and their derring-
do like Tarzan and Jane
in a Weissmuller flick,
and before I could say 'don't!'
I was in the water, locomoting
with my dog-paws, caught
in the furious current, and about
to go ignominiously under,
when I felt a very adult
hand gripping me by the chin
and hauling me aboard, ending
my quixotic bid for glory –
on the day I almost drowned,
but didn't.

Jig

Whenever I hopped aboard
the barber chair at Cap's
establishment, he'd chuck me
under the chin and squeeze
my knees just to hear
my giggle, and those were the days
when a chucked chin or a squeezed
knee meant nothing more,
and touch as such deemed
no more sordid
than Figaro's jig.

Budding Stud

Sarnia Township: 1949

I follow Marilyn and the sisters
Laur into her stable
to watch the resident stallion
"cover" his first mare,
and we notice he's ready to roll:
his pincering instrument as red
as a ripened rose and bigger
than an embalmed salami, and while
the sisters titter and Marilyn
is merely amused, the budding
stud straddles his inamorata
like an underrehearsed acrobat
and buries his sizzling implement
in the mare's mallow with stiff-
legged thrusts that leave
the girls a-gasp at such a
lacerating passion, and me
to wonder aloud about the
limits of lust, and us.

Addlepation

It's little wonder we kids
were perplexed at the lexicon
of our betters – when my inebriate
uncle was called to account:
"He's had a snootful!" or "Three
sheets to the wind he was!"
or "Plastered" vying with "Pie-
eyed!" and "Drunk as a skunk!"
seeming to say it all
in one clipped couplet –
and when we watched, with a guilt-
gnawing awe, our near-
neighbour stagger home
from closing time, something
forsook in his crooked glance,
I wondered which of those
offending epithets (and the guffaws
they raised) might best apply,
and whether there were words
enough in the language to describe
such an addlepated stare
and its less-than-human look.

Summer Sundays

Point Edward: 1947

Every Summer Sunday,
sun-shining Sabbath
or otherwise, Grandfather
marched a military mile
to keep his heart humming
and his blood in full flood,
and once in two blue
moons, I joined his parade,
stretching my strut to keep
in touch with his soldier's stride
and, arms swinging in rhythm,
we passed the cenotaph
where the names of long-ago
battles and the faithful fallen
are etched stalwart in stone
like a hieroglyphics of war
or the budded Braille of remembrance,
and we gave it a silent salute,
and walked on by the Slip
where sailboats dipped
their jibs into the witting wind,
and on it was to Canatara
and its drumlin-ed dunes, hewn
out of sand that Noah might've
poached for his beast-bloated
boat, and circling back
like pigeons drawn to the roost
that reared them, we addressed
the dappled dark of First Bush
and let its shadows have
their say, and soon found
ourselves home-aboded
where I said a wordless prayer
to the gilded gods for the gift
of such a day.

Harvesting Heaven

Chatham, Ontario: 1953

I had just turned sixteen,
as randy as a harlot in a harem,
with an itch to drive our two-
toned hardtop till the
whitewalls withered or the girls
weakened, and when my father
suggested I escort one of the
party-goers rocking
their socks in the rec-room
below, too liquored to be sick,
I played chauffeur to milady,
a blowsy, bloated blonde
whose eyes were too glazed
to blink or bat their lashes,
and we sat side by side,
unthinking in the dark,
until, safely parked,
I was stunned to feel a pair
of female fingers slither
on my thigh, and though my id
was aroused, this was not
the way I planned to harvest
"Heaven," or turn seventeen.

Nag

Sarnia Township: 1949

When I was still a lad,
every kid I knew
would kill for a pony at Christmas,
preferably a shaggy Shetland,
and Marilyn up the road
found one browsing under
her Tree, and we watched in
envious awe as she galloped it
by, biting the bit
in her white-knuckled grip,
its mane aflame, and while
I was praising her blue-eyed
pluck, Coop said,
with his usual, withering wit,
"That's quite a nag, and one
lucky dame."

Precise

Point Edward: 1946

Every afternoon at precisely
five-twenty-five,
whatever the season or its
reason, the Widow Bray's
dog, Bud, second
cousin to a Great Dane
and too thin for his skin,
would waddle across the road
and negotiate the lilac-hedge,
dragging his dewlaps with him,
whereupon he would find
awaiting his approval, a gravied
plate my Gran had salvaged
from Grandpa's supper, and out
would come his talented tongue,
like an adder's tasting the air
for its tang, and lap it up
with a juddering of jowl – and I
wondered, even then,
what kind of clock ticked
behind that conniving brow
to tickle his hunger at precisely
five-twenty-five.

Best Friends

For Butch McCord

When we decided to leave town
for the countryside, my best
friend, Butch, who kept
the bullies at bay in our school-
yard scrimmaging, and let me
cheat at Chinese checkers,
hopped aboard his CCM
and essayed to follow the van
as it wove its way thru the maze
of big-city streets
until he ran out of breath
or grit, and watched me
and our second-hand chattel
make an anguished exit
at the next bend and, like me,
vowing never to have a
new best friend.

Intimation

Point Edward: 1947

Death is merely a word
till it comes knocking at your door,
and I lived four doors
and an around-the-corner from the
spot where five-year-old
Effie Free danced
her last breath, and she was
such an elfin lass,
such a pigtailed pixie,
I could not think her
unalive, but there she lay
on the empty road like a
dropped doll, its pink
frillies primly propped
above the knees, while the car
that killed her kept wheezing
exhaust, and something
inside me gave way,
more shattering than shock.

Adonis

Point Edward: 1945

Bill Bray, who lived
over the road with his widowed
Mum, mowed the 'back
forty' of Grandfather's lawn
for four bits and a tip
of the hat every Saturday
the sun shone, his torso
bared and rippling sweat,
and I let my eight-year
eyes alight on this
bronzed Adonis, who might have
run the race to Marathon
or spoiled the Spartan's day
at Thermopylae, or posed
for a statue in Athens, and O
how I longed to be unyoung
and grip that grass machine
like Heracles, the golden
apples of the Hesperides
or perhaps a lone assassin,
his gun, but when the mowing
ceased, Bill was still
his Mum's boy and the Saturday
sun shone on.

Fetching

For Marybelle Cooper

Coop's cousin, Marybelle,
leaning into the light that haloed
our white picket-fence,
was as fetching
as Venus on the half-shell,
as Cinderella enthralling a Ball,
as Helen embroiling Troy,
as Guinevere captivating Camelot,
as Juliet embroidering a balcony —-
and left me as love-struck
as Lancelot (doting
where he shouldn't) or as lecherous
as Pan in his goat-footed
dance.

Tiptoed

Point Edward: 1945

The Missus Bradley stands
tiptoed on her front stoop,
as if she may need to run
or duck, but when the breeze
fails to buckle, and the sun
still bodes remote,
she lets the cry that threatens
to throttle in her throat, die.

Alleged

Chatham, Ontario: 1954

O how I envied my friend,
Jim, year younger
but not a wit wiser,
wedged behind the wheel
of the 48 Ford
he'd "borrowed" from his Dad's auto-
lot, and drove us up
and down the main drag
of our dusty town – in second
gear just to hear
the grind or put a jig
in the girls' giggle as we swept
on by like a pair of paladins
looking for something to shoot,
and on our second sally,
a blonde with too many curls
waved and winked, and Jim
said, with vigorous vim
and a pat on his privates, "I'd like
to put a dimple in that,"
and from where I sat, I couldn't
tell if the lust in his laugh
was real, or alleged.

Abaft

Chatham, Ontario: 1954

My friend, Jim, whose big
brown eyes with their bedroom
bent, made something jig
in the girls' giggle as he swept
on by them in his borrowed Ford,
one hand wisping the wheel
and the other draped agape
his latest snag, as if
he were reprising some scene
from *American Graffiti* – and O
the joy when he let me ride
abaft with his date's mate
all the way to a shaded lane,
where Jim happily harassed
his doxy's locks and whispered
nothings in the nearest ear,
while my "inamorata" and I
were parked primly in the pauper's
pew, a yard apart in the
condoning dark, embarrassed
at being embarrassed.

Beginning

While the girls "skinned the cat"
on the iron railings that skirted
our country school, the boys
romped on the back forty,
juggling a rugby-ball
between pediatric bursts
of speed, and we needed no-one
to tell us that these were the days
when the blood hummed and the heart
hammered heroic, and we were
boys-and-girls still
at home in the abode of our bones
with summer tucked inside –
unamazed at the din of our beginning.

Leckies' Barn

In Ted Leckies' abandoned
barn, devoid now
of cows or any other
bovine denizens, we hear
the purred murmuring of pigeons
in the bolstered beams above,
and through the cracks, where the wood
has withered, the noontide sun
festoons, and in the air
over the musty mow,
a million myriad motes
float, and something here
is more than magical, reminiscing
for the mind another further
stable, where cattle caught
the awe in their breath, and Magi
leaned and listened, and a Babe
was Bethlehem-born.

Fugue

For Tom in loving memory

O how we loved Raffi!
the way his syllables danced
and his rollicking rhymes chimed,
and there was a giggle in the mirth
of his music that left you
laughing out loud,
and whenever I hoisted the volume
to give "Baby Beluga"
a boost, we sang along,
our voices blended with his
in a furious child-wild
fugue.

Hallowed

Grandfather's house had already
stood sturdy for more
than a century when I arrived
for my eleven-year ride:
aging sandstone, double-
bricked to outwit the weather;
two verandahs, a front
and a side, so there was always
somewhere to sit in the shade;
a sun-swept wall
where ivy winced its annual
inch; a lilac hedge,
combed mauve in the May
mornings; two tall
trees where squirrels scurried
and evening breezes careened;
and a back forty big enough
to lengthen my lope – and even
though no poem had yet
puckered a page, this
hallowed ground was buckled
bright in every line
I unhitched from Heaven.

Original Sin

Did Adam wince when God
ripped a random rib
from his manly chest, and was
he surprised when that only bone
metamorphosed, and there
were two to romp like toddlers
thru the green leafage of Eden,
their private parts not yet
rudely protruding, and because
they had no thought of the joys
of joint-engendering, might not
we say they were committing
the sin of innocence?

Homing

Sarnia Township: 1950

Kenny LeNeve, new
to the neigbourhood, invites me
to admire the dovecote
he's built and peopled with pigeons,
and we watch their fevered flutter
or the way they sometimes bill
and coo like lisping lovers,
and when he releases them to the
eddying air, I sound
the alarm, but Kenny smiles
and says, "We'll see," and no sooner
are they a purple blur
on the far horizon, than,
cued by an instinct more urgent
than hunger or the yen to roam,
they come about like boats
afloat and head for home.

Resurrection

It was so humid that Sabbath
when they rolled the stone away,
unbrushed as it was by any
condoling breeze, that the bees,
hung with honey, hovered
in their hives, and gave up
their buzz for the nip-of-nectar,
and Missus Bray's blooms,
sun-tugged tulip
or deep-rooted daisy,
droop, sympathetic
in the heathen heat, and when
the dark comes down,
she prays for a righteous rain,
and the Resurrection.

Hoops

For Alfred Reeve in memoriam

My great-uncle, Alf,
took his brand-new
Ford coupe for a trial
run on Front Street,
where the traffic would've baffled
a hell-driver, and, giddy
with the spice of speed and assuming
the white line down the middle
was there as an aid to his aim,
he straddled it, and wondered why
everyone else was addled.
enough to lean on their horns
like indignant pygmies, and when
at last he made it home
(on the second attempt), unscathed
and auto-proud, he winked
at my aunt, and said, "I ran
hoops 'round the lot of 'em."

The Last Word

For my son, John

You snap this photo of me
standing in front of my Gran's
verandah and the home
where I roamed the kitchen
linoleum in toddler's togs
with barefoot bravado
and chinned my littler self
on the window ledge to let
the world amaze or grow
agog – now housing some
other I do not want
to know, for the gods allow us
to graze the hallowed ground
of childhood but once, and only
one room at a time
may halo in the dark womb
of a heart – but undeterred,
I smile as the shutter clicks:
the poet posing for posterity
or the last word.

Walkabout with My Son

Point Edward – June 19, 2022

So here we go walkabout
once again in the village
I kept hostage in my mind
for more than seventy years,
and plumbed its friendly purviews
for homegrown odes
and poems beatifying the joys
of boyhood and being
young enough to know better,
and these houses, slicked up
with fresh siding and shingles
and a patina of sweating paint,
still have the ring of recognition,
and as we amble from one
to another, I name the family
who'd nested therein, and the kids
I'd played with or didn't,
and we come at last to Grand-
father's house, double-
bricked against the eroding
appetite of Time (the aging
verandahs, leaning just
as they did when I preened
on them for passersby)
the abode where I was fostered
and fed and prompted to stalk
the streets and alleyways
and peopled precincts for words
to make up my world in rhythms
and rhyme.

One More Time

The Prince of Poetry Reading
June 25th, 2022

The aging poet does not
pose behind a podium
to project some bardic bravado,
he is seated, rather, in his walker,
awkwardly, as if he can feel
his bones brooding in their sockets,
and, wincing at "prince,"
he gathers what remains of his versifying
voice, glances at the words
swimming on the page below,
and begins, one more time,
to recite the lines still
marauding in his mind, hoping
against hope to find
the reason behind his rhymes
or a condoning abode for his poems –
content, this day, to let
the erotic of applause be enough.

Iceman

When I was six or seven
and Heaven awaited the faithful,
I wanted, when I grew big
enough for my britches, to be
an iceman, like the one who loped
lopsided down our walk
with a fifty-pound block,
tonged and tamed, in his five-
fingered grip, and I loved
the way the ice wobbled
with shards of sunlight shivering
inside, and got itself slung
up into the big kitchen-
box, where it dripped in the dark
to keep our goodies chilled,
as we raced to the truck, popped
slivers of chipped ice
onto our tongues, and let them
glide.

The Dance of Dialogue

My dear Aunt Let
pretended to be harder-of-
hearing than she really was,
opting to sit unremarked
in a corner of the kitchen, tremble-
lipped and teary-eyed,
ignored by others in the room
for whom dialogue was a daily
dance – hoping she might elicit
sympathy or prompt some
gossiping goose to come
over and drum the news
thru the deaf weft in her head,
but till then, the only sound
to tickle the silence humming
inside her was the impudent
squeal of the maladjusted
instrument, unused in her ear.

Ambling

For Tom in loving memory

You and I, ambling
the manicured meadows
of the local links, happy
just to be walking together
thru the amber-hued afternoon,
and whenever your drive feathers
a fairway, you give me
a grin, as if to say,
"Did I really do that again?"
and up ahead, on the beige
acre of the green, when your putt
is cradled by the cup, you look
at me and wink, and I nod
my unsurprise, and it's days
like this when souls synthesize
that are a gift from the gods,
who've decided for once
to let their envy unabide.

No Surprise

Uncle Alf and Aunt Let
invariably arrived in the late
afternoon of Christmas Day,
long after Bob and I
had gorged ourselves on gifts
from Santa and his gelded elves,
and the blue-ribboned boxes
they proferred with avuncular verve,
looked much like slim lozenges
that might have housed pin-
striped ties or a monogrammed
hanky, but when we unbuttoned them,
there was never the shock of surprise
or the squeal of O-gosh-delight,
for as long as turkey was noshed
at Christmas dinner or stars
brimmed more brightly
on Noel night and there were
uncles and aunts to spare,
we'd get a prim pair
of double-diamond Argyle
socks, and smile.

On the Level

For Great-Aunt Let and Great-Uncle Alf:
in loving memory

My Great-Aunt Let,
fearful of hills and everything
else, would sit, tight-
lipped and finger-wrung
beside my uncle while he drove them
to visit Great-Granny
Reeve, whose cottage perched
on the upper half of a slow
slope, and going up
gave neither shock nor shiver
to Let's fettle, but when
it came time, heading
home, to brave the gradient,
my aunt baulked at the top,
stepped out of the car,
and walked warily to the bevel's
bottom, where life was on
the level.

Boogie

For my brother, Bob, in loving memory

No-one remembers who
christened you "Googie"
after some cartoon stooge
in the funny papers, but the
sobriquet stuck, and even
your mother probably forgot
she'd named you "Robert,"
and Googie you were throughout
the town, and answered to no
other, although, deep down,
something about the ooga-
ooga timbre of that mis-
begotten moniker throbbed
wrongly, because the minute
we'd settled our names and our noggins
in the countryside, you introduced
yourself to all and sundry
as "Bob," and boogied with it
the rest of the way.

A-Brim

For Tim

And you, barely five,
at the top of the block, tugging
free of your mother's hovering
hand, and me doing
my best to remain unfluttered
a hundred yards below,
and when Grandma gives you
the sign, you toddle down
the walk with little stutter-
steps, like a junior jockey
or a loose-limbed marionette
hugging the limelight,
and you're no more than a
dozen paces away
when your eyes brim with a
beatific delight and a smile
that says, "See, this
is what love does."

Remembering When

Point Edward: 1947-2022

It's been more than seventy
years since I was a lad,
hopping from toe to toe
here in Lorne Hillier's
soda shop with a dime
cupped in my pocket that would buy me
a double-dip, and even though
there are now a dozen flavours
of ice cream under this
gleaming glass façade
and the room around it has been
dazzled blue and white,
I still expect the man
himself to step out from behind
the counter and hand me
a chocolate cone with his custom
smile, and set me once
again – remembering when.

Don Gutteridge was born in Sarnia and raised in the nearby village of Point Edward. He taught High School English for seven years, later becoming a Professor in the Faculty of Education at Western University, where he is now Professor Emeritus. He is the author of more than seventy books: poetry, fiction and scholarly works in pedagogical theory and practice. He has published twenty-two novels, including the twelve-volume Marc Edwards mystery series, and forty-nine books of poetry, one of which, Coppermine, was short-listed for the 1973 Governor-General's Award. In 1970 he won the UWO President's Medal for the best periodical poem of that year, "Death at Quebec." Don lives in London, Ontario.

Email: gutteridgedonald@gmail.com.